MASTER YOUR MIND

HOW TO CONTROL YOUR MENTAL STATE INSTEAD OF YOUR MENTAL STATE CONTROLLING YOU

LOGAN D. BRYANT

Copyright © 2020 by Logan D. Bryant.

Master Your Mind: *How to Control Your Mental State Instead of Your Mental State Controlling You*

All rights reserved. No part of this publication may be reproduced, distributed or transmitted in any form or by any means, including photocopying, recording, or other electronic or mechanical methods, without the prior written permission of the publisher, except in the case of brief quotations embodied in critical reviews and certain other noncommercial uses permitted by copyright law.

Although the author and publisher have made every effort to ensure that the information in this book was correct at press time, the author and publisher do not assume and hereby disclaim any liability to any party for any loss, damage, or disruption caused by errors or omissions, whether such errors or omissions result from negligence, accident, or any other cause.

Adherence to all applicable laws and regulations, including international, federal, state and local governing professional licensing, business practices, advertising, and all other aspects of doing business in the US, Canada or any other jurisdiction is the sole responsibility of the reader and consumer.

Neither the author nor the publisher assumes any responsibility or liability whatsoever on behalf of the consumer or reader of this material. Any perceived slight of any individual or organization is purely unintentional.

The resources in this book are provided for informational purposes only and should not be used to replace the specialized training and professional judgment of a health care or mental health care professional.

Neither the author nor the publisher can be held responsible for the use of the information provided within this book. Please always consult a trained professional before making any decision regarding treatment of yourself or others.

ISBN: 978-1-7361209-0-3

Printed in the United States of America.

Interior Design by FormattedBooks.com

This book is dedicated to my wife, Tory, for supporting me no matter what path I choose.

"Who you are, what you think, feel, and do, what you love—is the sum of what you focus on."

—CAL NEWPORT, DEEP WORK: RULES FOR FOCUSED SUCCESS IN A DISTRACTED WORLD

TABLE OF CONTENTS

Foreword ix
Introduction xi
Meet Your Brain 1
Train Your Puppy 7
Build Good Habits 19
Learn the Basics 23
Zero to Hero—Where to Start 29
Meditation is a Real Thing 37
Transferring Your Mental Strength 43
The Beta Brain 47
The Negative Effects of Beta State 55
Structure Your Day Around Your Brainpower 61
You Need to Calm Down 65
Transitioning into Unconsciousness—The Theta State 69
Success Happens Overnight—The Delta State 73
Putting It All Together 81
The Eureka State 83
Where to Go from Here 93
Additional Reading 103
Acknowledgments 105
About the Author 107

FOREWORD

This book is about your brain. But this small section is about *why* this book is about your brain.

It's obvious that there is tension in our country right now. I don't even need to give examples.

If you're like me, you want to help guide this country to a better future. But the more I thought about it, the more I realized I had no clue where to start.

I needed to look within. How do I find out what I truly believe? How do I arrive at a fundamental truth? How can I find something that I can hold on tight to, without doubt that I am right?

I'm not religious, but I was searching for a religious type of conviction.

I looked at what all humans had in common. I looked at what causes us to form our opinions, what causes our emotions, and what causes our suffering and happiness. I saw how this process was manipulated, and so I wanted to learn how we can learn to control this process for ourselves.

The answer to these issues is understandably complex. Every time I asked "why," or "how," I peeled back another layer of the onion, until I eventually landed on a commonality shared by all humans: the brain.

The brain is the lens through which every human being sees the world. There is no experience without it.

Your brain makes up your entire being. It makes up your consciousness, your thoughts, your emotions, and your opinions. And while someone else's opinions may be different than yours, their brain chemistry works in a similar manner. You cannot learn to understand why others make the decisions that they do until you understand their mind.

But before you learn to understand someone else's mind, you should get to know your own.

In short, if you want to make an impact, you should understand your own mind inside and out.

Learn to know yourself before you attempt to know others.

That's why this book is about your brain.

INTRODUCTION

Back when you were in college, did you ever hear the words *you can't wait until the last minute to start this paper*?

If you're like me, you'd then do exactly that, waiting until the very last possible second to write a ten-page paper, submitting it at 11:59PM in a caffeine (or Adderall) fueled bender.

But this approach is not optimal. Nobody *likes* doing this.

If you have this problem, then you've probably tried to be one of those normal people who can do work on a regular schedule. But you can't. You'll get started—sit down at your computer, get ready to write and you just can't.

Suddenly you've spent 6 hours mindlessly scrolling through various apps on your phone, unconsciously hoping that something in one of those little boxes will make you slightly happier than you would be if you were working.

I originally thought I was the only one with this problem. But it turns out, the people who actually do their work on time are the weird ones: the average millennial spends 5.7 hours a day on their phone.

If this is you, you know it's a miserable limbo to be stuck in. You have the inability to be productive, but you also have the inability to relax without feeling guilty for what you should be doing.

The logical part of your brain wants you to get all of your shit done so you can move on to something else, whether it be something productive or guilt free relaxation. But there's another part of your brain dragging you in a different direction.

If you extrapolate this pattern out for the rest of your life, you realize that your conscious brain—the one that sets goals, has dreams, and wants to make your life better—is only getting its way a small percentage of the time. There's another part of your brain dragging you down this path of misery.

If you're spending a lot of time stuck in this feedback loop, are you really even in charge of your own life? Do you control the thoughts that are in your head, or are you letting another part of your subconscious brain control you? And if you're letting your subconscious brain control you... who controls your subconscious brain? (*hint... usually someone trying to sell you something*).

If you don't put a stop to this, you'll be 80 years old, and will have spent at least half of your productive life stuck between productivity and relaxation. Imagine what you could have done with that time.

Not even just the productive time; think about all the time you should've been productive, but instead you were fucking off, and then you're forced to be productive later that evening. Or on a weekend. If you don't fix this habit, you're not only lowering the impact you could make on the world, you're now spending less time with your friends, and over the years less time with your children, because your subconscious brain had control over your schedule and your consciousness was only able to take control up against an impending deadline.

It's not a loop you want to be stuck in. But the longer you're stuck in the loop, the longer it takes to get out of it.

You need to work on getting out now. This book will tell you how, but it's up to you to actually do it.

Learning how your brain works and implementing a system to get back on track will be the biggest productivity boost you'll ever get. It's bigger than coffee. It's bigger than prescription ADHD medicine. It's bigger than impending deadlines. Those are just Band-Aids—this is a cure. And the cure isn't just for productivity. It's balance.

Balance between work, relaxation, family, routine, sleep, exercise—all of the things you want to do but feel like you never have time for.

If I had to give it to you in one sentence, it's this—take a few months to work with your brain and you won't be able to recognize who you were at the start of your journey.

I could spend the next 12 pages telling you what this book can do for you and how it will do it. But your subconscious makes decisions quickly—much faster than your conscious mind. You decided if you were going to keep reading after the first nine seconds whether you knew it or not.

Let's get started.

MEET YOUR BRAIN

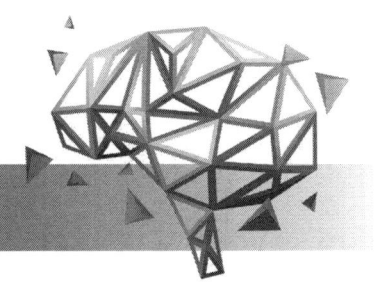

K nowing how your brain works is fundamental to, well, literally everything. Working, eating, sleeping, daydreaming; the one constant in every experience you've had or will ever have is your brain. Your brain is the operating system that connects your conscious being to the hardware that enables you to experience the world around you.

No matter what form of procrastination you choose, whether you're scrolling through your phone, or if you've taken it up a level to "productive procrastination," (think, *I cleaned my house and did laundry instead of this work project...*) a subconscious part of your brain is dragging your actions away from the goals set by your conscious brain.

I want you to think of this part of your brain as a little puppy.

And just like a puppy, if left unattended, it will find mischief, and the owner (the conscious brain), will be chasing after it. But if properly trained, it can be a lifelong companion.

Your inner puppy is just one of five parts of your brain. Technically your puppy isn't a part of your brain, it's really parts of your brain working together on one frequency. Let me explain:

> We humans have this tendency to break things down into their component parts to understand them. Everything we've ever studied—math, reading, atoms, the periodic table of elements—it all gets broken down so we can understand what each little piece does. For the longest time, we did the same thing with the brain.

In 1848, a guy named Phineas Gage caused an explosion, and an iron rod went through the roof of his mouth and out the top of his skull. Miraculously, he survived, but his personality was changed forever, creating the first human brain experiment: "This is what happens when you remove a piece of the brain."

For the next 100 years, to learn about the brain all we could really do was observe what happened to miraculous survivors of similar accidents. Some unethical experiments were performed on mentally ill psych patients, but the extent of the experimentation was "remove one part of the brain, see what happens." For obvious reasons, these experiments weren't performed often, or on healthy people.

It was a conundrum—how do we learn what the brain does without damaging it? If we open it up, we break it. But we have no way to see what it does without opening it up.

In recent years, we've found that the brain doesn't really work like this; brain function isn't the result of one part of the brain doing one thing. Sure, certain brain areas have dominant control over certain processes, but your thought processes are a result of all of the pieces working together simultaneously. The whole is greater than the sum of its parts. Like any robust system, a single part can't fulfill the entire purpose.

And when all of those pieces work together in tandem, your brain emits electrical signals (roughly enough to power an LED light bulb). A pretty awesome piece of technology called an electroencephalogram (EEG) is capable of measuring the electrical signals that flow between the different parts of your brain.

Every thought you've ever had is the result of electrical signals flowing across your neurons, from one brain area to the next. These signals can be broken down into five patterns based on their frequency— each frequency known as a "brain wave."

The more active and excited your brain is, the higher the frequency of your brain waves will be. Your brain waves fall into one of the five following states, and learning to control what state you're in is the key to taking control over your actions:

- Delta Waves - Frequency: 0–4 Hz. Delta waves are the slowest brainwaves and are displayed strongly when you're in a period of deep, dreamless sleep. If you're dreaming, you're not in a delta brain state. You experience delta waves when your thinking brain is shut off, and the most primitive part of your brain is hard at work healing the day's stress on your body.

- Theta Waves - Frequency: 4–8 Hz. Theta waves occur most often during dream sleep, but can also be found in the brains of experienced meditators. Waking theta waves are most associated with deeply ingrained habits or periods of deep relaxation. Think back to a time before cell phones—do you remember a time when you were simply staring off into space and snapped out of it, and had no clue what you were thinking about? Those were probably theta waves.
- Alpha Waves - Frequency 8–13 Hz. Alpha brainwaves are found in an alert, yet relaxed brain state. Good examples of alpha thought are simple reading, yoga, or going on a mindful walk. You're not solving complex problems, but you aren't asleep. You're just present.
- Beta Waves - Frequency 13–32 Hz. Beta brainwaves are found during intense periods of concentration. You're in a beta state when you're writing, thinking hard about a problem, or when you're active in conversation or making decisions. Beta waves are best known for "difficult" thought. Prolonged periods of beta brain activity can be utterly exhausting.

- Gamma Waves - Frequency 32–100 Hz. Gamma waves are found during peak concentration and high levels of brain function. Gamma waves are the most difficult to detect and they tend to be fleeting, but they have been associated with times when all areas of the brain are firing at once; think "eureka" moments.

Every thought and emotion you have lies within one of these brain states. And as much as you would like to, you can't force yourself to live within one of them. You must find the correct balance between all five.

Once you learn to recognize your current brain state, you can teach yourself to move between them. If you've learned to recognize when you're in a beta brain state, and you've taught yourself how to move down to an alpha state, you can learn to control your emotions.

Anger, panic, and anxiety are all beta state emotions. The mind is going a mile a minute, and hundreds of thoughts are flying into your head. If you're anything like me, you don't make good decisions when you're angry. But if you've learned to recognize anger, and you've practiced de-escalating your brain from beta to alpha state hundreds of times, you can say:

"I'm sorry, just give me five minutes."

You can go through the process, and you can return to the conversation in alpha state.

Let's talk about how.

TRAIN YOUR PUPPY

Every effective person out there knows that good habits are essential. But I've read every single book on habits, and none of them really nail the neuroscience behind why they're so important.

It's because your beta brain gets tired.

A strong beta brain makes you an effective person, but your beta brain gets exhausted pretty quickly. Throughout your day, your beta brain makes thousands of decisions, and the more decisions it makes, the harder it is to make the next one. Eventually you burn out. This burnout is called "decision fatigue."

One study on decision fatigue analyzed the decisions made by judges in granting parole to incarcerated persons. Prisoners who appeared early in the morning received parole about 70% of the time, while those who appeared late in the day were paroled less than 10% of the time. The conductors of the study controlled for factors that would account for a prisoner being granted parole and found that there was no meaningful difference between the morning and afternoon prisoners regarding whether they were truly deserving of parole. So why such a big difference in outcome?

Because the judge was exhausted by 4 p.m. It was easy for them to fall into a pattern and not consciously think about their decisions, and when this happens, the brain opts for the default choice. Here, the default was denial of parole. For you, the default after a morning of fatiguing decisions might be scrolling through your phone.

The more important decisions you have to make in a day, the more important it is that you cut down on decision fatigue. Brilliant people understand this. Steve Jobs, Mark Zuckerberg, and Barack Obama chose to wear the same outfit every day so they had one less decision to make.

The easiest way to fight decision fatigue is to cut down on the decisions you have to make every day. How? Turn decisions into habits.

This works because when you turn a decision into a habit, you're no longer making a decision. The decision is made for you. You're freeing up space in the beta brain to make more important decisions, because the things you do every single day are on autopilot. They're systematized. You do the same thing, at the same time, every single day.

The key to having a more effective beta brain—to being laser focused at work, decision making, and deep, concentrated thought—lies in having an incredibly powerful alpha brain that runs the rest of your life on a system. In short, you need to train your puppy to be your personal assistant.

You can do this by hijacking the part of your brain that controls your bad habits and steering it toward good ones.

"Okay, I want to teach my brain to systematize daily actions. I want to build habits. But my inner puppy has some bad habits and is dragging me around. Where do I start?"

If you're a human, I'm 100% certain that you have a bad habit.

The key to breaking a bad habit is knowing how they were formed in the first place. Most people never analyze this; suddenly they're mindlessly repeating an action that isn't good for them. Understanding how bad habits are formed is the key to replacing them with good habits.

For our purposes, we'll define a bad habit as anything on autopilot that detracts from your long-term quality of life. Bonus points if the secondary goal is to seek short-term pleasure.

I want you to think about a bad habit you have. (That second part can get a bit argumentative—if your bad habit has become an *addiction* you will find yourself rationalizing that it is *not* detracting from your long-term quality of life.) Pick something simpler than that for this example.

If you couldn't tell, my biggest bad habit was (and still is) cell phone use. It's something I don't consciously choose to do—I just reach for my phone out of habit and start checking notifications. If I'm out of notifications, I start scrolling. Facebook, Instagram, Snapchat, it doesn't matter. "I'll get back to work at noon," I tell myself.

"Shit, how is it 1 p.m.?"

This is a classic bad habit. Most people would agree that mindless cell phone use does not add to one's quality of life, and I get the bonus points, because notifications definitely cause short-term pleasure. The experience of receiving a Facebook notification shows similar functions in your brain to a gambling addict.

But I digress. Hopefully you've chosen a bad habit. Whether it's mindlessly checking your phone, swinging through the drive through, binging trashy TV, or online shopping, you've got a bad habit.

How did we get here? How did this simple action get so engrained into our brains?

Well, the first time we experienced our bad habit, it was a choice.

Our bad habits started as high-energy, beta brain activity, and through repeated action became alpha activity. Some habits are so engrained in us that they even become theta-brain activity; closer to a dream state and being performed without any awareness. As you performed an action over and over, it became easier and easier, and less of a conscious decision.

The bad habit you chose—do you remember the very first time you tried it? If it's been engrained in you for a long time, maybe you don't. But for me, I can still remember the very day I activated my Facebook account.

Twelve years ago—back in 2008 when the "Facebook timeline" was still called the "Facebook Wall," I logged on for the first time to talk to my friends. I've always been an extrovert, so I was thrilled to have social interaction available to me within my home.

This new level of excitement that came with the new experience was full of beta activity. My thoughts were running a mile a minute. *Who's online now? Who can I talk to? How do I get more Facebook friends? More likes?*

I was actively thinking about it. I was putting effort into it. It was fun and exciting, and every little red notification came with a flood of dopamine. *Someone wants to talk to me. Look, friends!* My instant happiness level went up a notch.

The first time you experienced your bad habit, your brain was actively consuming it. All of your brain parts were working in tandem. Your logical, beta-level brain was making active decisions to pursue more, feeding information to your reward center. Your beta brain then made a conscious decision to pursue more of that reward. You most likely pondered the good feelings and thought about what actions you could take to achieve more of them.

Each time you repeated the action though, the system got more efficient. The brain learns that the same actions lead to the same results, and it only has one LED lightbulb worth of power. The brain has to stay efficient. If it sees an action being performed over and over, it will systematize it.

That original pathway of neurons—from the decision center to the movement of your eyes and hand, to the reward center—starts carving a highway in your brain.

As time went on, you fell into a cycle. Action, anticipation of reward, fulfillment of that reward.

No matter what bad habit you have, the cycle is the same.

Anticipate the reward of a notification. Post on Facebook. Receive notification, fulfilling the anticipation.

Anticipate the taste of food. Pull in the drive through. Eat the food, fulfilling the anticipation.

Anticipate the payout of a slot machine. Pull the handle. Receive payout. (Plot twist; it gets even more addicting if payouts are unpredictable).

After repeating this cycle 10,000 times, you're not making decisions anymore. The cars driving on your mental highway are on autopilot. You don't need to consciously tell your eyes or your arm what to do. You don't even think about what you're doing anymore—it's completely automated.

Anticipation. Action. Reward. Anticipation. Action. Reward.

What bad habit did you choose? Does it follow the same cycle? Do you anticipate a reward, take an action to fulfill that reward, and then receive the reward? Finally, have you repeated it hundreds if not thousands of times, to the point where you are no longer consciously choosing to start the cycle?

Is it on autopilot?

The brain's process of placing things on autopilot is a result of what neuroscientists call "neuroplasticity," or the brain's ability to optimize the neural roads between brain centers in order to find the path of least resistance.

Your brain has evolved to cut out the effort and reduce the redundancy. It wants to be more efficient. If you do something every single day, it wants to cut out as much effort as possible to free up more room.

It's been doing this since you were born. An example of how constant this process is may shed some light: did you know that the day you were born, you couldn't actually see? Babies aren't blind, their eyes take in light, but their brain doesn't know what that light is. They don't know what they're seeing, they just get an immediate shock of … light, because the infant brain hasn't even developed to a point to interpret color yet.

The sensory input of the light has to travel through the baby's eyes, then bounce around in the brain, because the brain doesn't have any conscious experience to compare that light to. When your eyes see light, your brain can interpret that light as having reflected off a surface of a certain color, which you have experienced to be a cup of coffee, or a kitchen chair. But a baby has never even experienced color; the baby doesn't know how to differentiate it.

But over time, the baby will touch a chair, and will see that when it looks at its hand next to the chair, the thing it's touching is a different color than what surrounds it. And when the thing on top of the chair moves, the baby can feel it (because the thing is the baby's hand).

Eventually, after doing this often enough, the baby can look at a chair and think, "This object is a different thing than my hand, and where the color changes, the object ends."

Every time this process is repeated, it gets more efficient. The brain begins carving a path of least resistance from the eye to the final destination in the brain. And eventually, this path is so solid, the baby (now a child) can see the chair, and just walk around it while on her way to grab a bite to eat, not even noticing that the chair is there.

By the time we hit adulthood, we've carved billions of neuroplastic pathways into our brain. Eating, walking, driving—there are thousands of things you do every day without thinking about them. Even reading this sentence is a result of neuroplastic pathways carved into your brain (unless you're still learning to read, then kudos to you for choosing this book).

The loop of anticipation, action, and reward will create these pathways for you. Our brains are programmed to make the decision to seek more of what provides us pleasure, and we will use the beta brain to consciously do so until the process is automated.

Except here's the problem: today, there's a disconnect between what our brain has evolved to reward us for and our ability to obtain those rewards.

Our brains haven't changed much in 2000 years. And 2000 years ago, your ancestors had to be rewarded mentally in order to seek out food, sex, and social interaction just to stay alive. The anticipation of those rewards drove humans to find the materials to continue our species. Without those rewards, our ancestors would have lacked the will to survive.

But when the rewards are abundant, the process stops leading to survival and starts leading to mental illness. Let's use food as an example.

Thousands of years ago our bodies evolved to reward us in the form of dopamine for eating food. The reward evolved out of the need for the person to survive.

But today, it's possible for humans to experience the same reward at their will without much effort. Food is everywhere. You can get food out of my fridge, in the restaurant below your apartment, at the store, in the drive through—the brain is still programmed to chase those rewards based on thousands of years of mental evolution, and neuroplasticity systemizes the decision-making required to fulfill my anticipation. Your brain then puts your ability to obtain food on autopilot.

But the brain isn't yet aware of the fact that we've learned to hack the reward pathway and have access to an endless amount of food, so it keeps unknowingly routing you toward the drive through, as if it thinks if you don't eat more food you'll starve.

For the sake of argument, let's assume that normal access to food results in a dopamine level of 10. When you eat food, the 10 dopamine-carrying neurons that travel across your mental pathways encounter 10 dopamine receptors. These receptors translate the 10 dopamine-carrying neurons into pleasure for eating food. The anticipation-action-reward pathway is fulfilled, and your brain says "more."

The brain has a certain amount of dopamine receptors available, and those dopamine receptors are calibrated to live in a world where food isn't so readily available. So, by the time you'd normally be able to get more, you would actually need it. A few centuries ago, the brain was balanced. But today, you can get more instantly. So you do. Now you have 20 dopamine-carrying neurons flooding your brain with pleasure for eating more food.

As time goes on, your brain adapts to this system by reducing the amount of dopamine receptors available to process pleasure, resulting in the need to consume *more* food to get the same amount of pleasure. You then need to continue flooding the system with 20 dopamine-carrying neurons to receive the same amount of pleasure that 10 used to give you. And if you really want enjoyment, maybe you'll indulge for food that gives you 30 hits of dopamine. But guess what? If you keep doing this, your brain will reduce your dopamine receptors again.

After months (or years) of repeating this cycle, your brain will have massively downregulated your dopamine receptors, and you'll be miserable. Why? Because it isn't just your one addiction that flows through your dopamine receptors, it is all activities that bring you pleasure.

If you're cramming enough food into your body to flood your dopamine receptors, and your receptors are reduced to a fifth of what they used to be to compensate, everything else that made you happy will now only make you a fifth as happy. If sunshine used to give you dopamine, well, you can't get more sunshine, and your brain will now only accept a fifth of the happiness it used to bring you.

This cycle repeats with anything that is readily available to us that creates dopamine. Food, drugs, sex, social media; excess use causes us to lose dopamine receptors, making everything else in our life that was once enjoyable less so, simply to compensate for our over-indulgence in the reward. Suddenly nothing makes you happy except an over-indulgence in one thing, and you chase more of it for pieces of happiness.

It's a downward spiral. And depending on your vice, it can take anywhere from 2-3 months (porn, food) to 2 years (hard drugs) for your dopamine receptors to return to a normal level.

Maybe in 10,000 years the rewards our brain produces for abundant objects will decrease as a product of evolution. But today, there is mismatch between reward and the ability to obtain those rewards that causes you to over-indulge in your habits to a point of unhealthy systemization.

In summary, your mental programming causes you to systematize short-term reward chasing to your detriment.

But, good news. You can take control of this system. You have advantages that all of your ancestors lacked—the knowledge of a century or two of science, and modern medicine that keeps you alive longer.

You can beat this cycle, but only if you choose to.

BUILD GOOD HABITS

Chasing short-term rewards kept our ancestors alive, but compounded, the effects of chasing those rewards have long-term consequences. Let's be honest, the human race has many flaws when it comes to long-term planning, but hopefully, if you're reading this book, you're looking for a way around that. You are wired for the short term, but you can re-wire for the long term.

Motivated people want to have an impact on the world. The simple math here is that those who change their bad habits into good ones tend to stay on this planet for a longer period of time, in the end having a much larger impact than those who keep their bad habits.

Centuries of doctors and medical experts have taught us what we need to do to stay around longer; now we just need to actually do it. But as we learned previously, making decisions and taking concrete actions is actually really hard, especially when our days are full of other stressful decisions.

So how do we overcome this? We systematize those actions—make them automatic—so we free up decision-making power to make an even bigger impact. How, when these bad habits are dragging you down?

It's incredibly hard to break a bad habit, because by definition, habits don't break. In this sense, your brain operates like the memory on a computer.

When you hit the "delete" button on a computer, the information stored in the computer's memory doesn't actually go away, it just becomes less easy to access, and a computer guru can still recover it. Once data is written into a memory drive, it can only be deleted if something else is written *over* it.

Your brain already contains the neuroplastic pathways to run on autopilot, and your brain is going to run a process on those pathways whether you like it or not. You can exercise all of the willpower you want to prevent it, but as you already know, your beta-brained willpower will deplete, and that super-highway will run again.

Something has to run on that pathway. So instead of using a ton of brainpower to try and run nothing, just use a little brain power to run something less harmful, and eventually, something helpful. In the end, the goal is that you've completely swapped a bad habit for a good one with your neuroplastic pathway running a circuit the entire time.

This is called *habit substitution*. It is why AA meetings are full of cigarette smokers, and why heroin addicts are given methadone to break the habit; it's always easier to substitute a slightly healthier habit for a really bad one. The easiest way to break a bad habit is to swap it out for a slightly less bad habit.

What we're doing here is taking conscious control over the "action" part of the system. In a bad habit, your brain really, really wants something and you take an action to fulfill that want, except you do it automatically. To create a good habit, you just kind of have to force the action consciously until it creates a system.

A bad habit forms over time because you repeat an action that feels good in the short term, your brain forms a system, and then in the long term, it has negative consequences.

A good habit is the inverse. You repeat an action that feels *bad* in the short term compared to the high of a bad habit—a 5a.m. workout feels a lot worse than a cold-brew coffee. But then in the long term, it starts to feel really, really good. Over time, the same thing happens. If you repeat the action over and over, your ever-efficient brain will build a system and put that action on autopilot. Taking the hard action will get easier.

Look at this path:

>Alcohol habit >> cigarette habit >>
>caffeine habit >> exercise habit.

Each of the above actions releases a set of endorphins into the brain, but we can all agree that each successive habit is healthier than the previous one. If you can slowly wean yourself off cigarettes and onto caffeine, you give your brain something to latch onto instead of the cigarettes. Then you can do the same thing for exercise.

LEARN THE BASICS

If you're training a puppy to do something, you simply repeat the action over and over and offer a reward for successful performance of the action. To train your own inner puppy, you can do the same thing.

Remember our goal is to substitute a good habit for a bad one. We're not trying to just create a good habit from scratch here. We're killing two birds with one stone and getting the double positive of killing off a bad habit and replacing it with a good one. This is actually easier than starting from scratch, because the neuroplastic pathway for the habit to run on already exists.

There are two ways to substitute a good habit for a bad one; you can go cold turkey, or you can ease into it.

Cold Turkey Switch

If you have a lot of willpower, you can go cold turkey and attempt to break a bad habit by immediately substituting a good one. It's up to you to make the determination about whether you're ready for it. Do you have enough brainpower saved up, or are you juggling multiple responsibilities and also trying to squeeze this in? If you have the brainpower, this method is faster. If you don't (and be honest with yourself, it's okay if you don't) you should choose the second method.

There are pros and cons to going cold turkey—the negative side is that if you're truly hooked on a bad habit and quit out of the blue, it's easy to fall back into it. On the plus side, you're just getting it over with, and you can say something along the lines of "I don't look at my phone before bed" instead of "I'm trying to stop." The psychological power of identifying with a trait is very powerful.

I once gained a bad habit of drinking a glass of wine before bed every night, and to successfully break it, I did a cold-turkey substitution. I had only been doing this for about a month, but I knew it could quickly get worse, so I immediately switched that habit over to LaCroix. LaCroix is undoubtedly healthier, but when I made this switch, I remember my wife commenting on how much LaCroix I drank in a week. I was drinking three to four cans a night.

When you go cold turkey, no matter what habit you have, you will experience some form of adjustment. It may be physical withdrawal, it could be something as innocent as just being a little grouchy, or just not feeling right, or maybe it's an over-commitment to your new habit.

The adjustment for me manifested as guzzling LaCroix. My alcoholic brain cells were chanting "WINE. WINE.

WINE," but I got them to shut up for a bit by chugging slightly fruity seltzer water. Why did this work?

Those dopamine hits we just discussed—you'd think your brain releases it when you get your fix, but no. It's really the anticipation of reward that sets off the chemicals in your brain, not the reward itself. In multiple experiments on addicts, neuroscientists have found that the brain area associated with reward is an absolute blast of activity right *before* and up to experiencing the reward, and not so much during.

The high a gambler experiences comes from the uncertainty of waiting for a big win, not the big win itself, and the bigger the uncertainty of a win, the bigger the high. This is why your cell phone games all have an uncertain gambling component, like spinning the wheel for a daily prize. It makes the game more addicting.

When you fulfill the anticipation, the brain takes a break for a bit. When I drank a glass of wine, the alcohol in it wouldn't have hit my brain cells for 10 to 15 minutes after drinking it, but the anticipation would've been soothed at the first sip. "We wanted it, we got it. The reward is coming, we can shut up," my brain cells say.

But my beta brain knew this and outsmarted my alpha brain system. I'd drink a can of LaCroix, and because the alcohol wouldn't have hit for about 15 minutes anyway, it would trick my brain into thinking the LaCroix was actually wine. But 30 minutes later, my alpha brain realized it had been tricked. So, I'd drink another can of LaCroix.

After two weeks though, the adjustment period was over. I was down to one can a night, and I had freed up that pathway for something else. Today my evening routine looks completely different.

Ease Into It

Your other option is to stack a good habit on top of a bad one, and then slowly wean yourself off the bad habit. As we speak, I am in the process of doing this with yoga and cell phone use.

My normal nightly habit is to just scroll through my phone before bed, which is bad because the blue light assaults my eyes, and the Facebook feed activates my beta-level brain—all bad for sleep. So, I started a nightly yoga habit, but I didn't stop the cell phone habit, I just stacked them.

Now, instead of looking at my phone for an hour, I do yoga for a half hour and look at my phone for a half hour. The pathway is still running at full capacity, and my brain isn't experiencing withdrawals.

After a month or so, my brain will start to associate yoga with that uncertain ping of anticipation related to social media addiction. My alpha-level brain will look forward to yoga just as much as cell phone use; but I've already cut my cell phone use in half. In another week, I'll cut it down to 15 minutes, and a week after that, hopefully none at all.

In the end, I will have slowly introduced a positive habit onto the same neuroplastic pathway as the bad habit, and with a little effort from the beta brain, I used the positive habit to shove the negative one out the door, all while maintaining the same bandwidth.

The negative side of slowly substituting a habit is that it's really easy to slide back into it. If you're looking at your phone for 30 minutes every night and trying to cut down to 15, are you really going to stop at 15 minutes? You need to make this decision for yourself.

Whether you're going cold turkey or easing into it, you can always be working with your brain to become more efficient and healthier.

ZERO TO HERO— WHERE TO START

You can follow this pattern of habit substitution until you're satisfied with your daily routine and no longer have any "bad" habits. Be patient with yourself; this takes a lot of time. You might even find that, after a few years, one of your "good habits" that you substituted out a few years ago is actually now "bad" compared to your new lifestyle. (I substituted caffeine for sleeping in, and now I'm questioning my caffeine dependence).

You (hopefully) now understand how bad habits are formed, and the science behind how habit substitution works. But there are a few more tricks to start living the life you want to live a little faster.

I don't need to completely reinvent the wheel. I learned a lot of this from two amazing books:

1. *The Power of Habit* by Charles Duhigg
2. *Atomic Habits* by James Clear

If you want to get 100% out of your brain, I highly suggest that you read both. But until then, here are a few crucial tips you shouldn't live without.

Start with an Atomic Habit

Atomic habits, keystone habits, waterfall habits, whatever you want to call them, you need to find one habit that you will never live without. This one habit should be unbreakable, no-holds barred, nothing will ever stop you from doing it. A lifestyle coach once told me that even on the day his mother died, he still did his atomic habit the next morning.

This may sound extreme, but your atomic habit is what grounds you. We humans are creatures of routine; routine makes us happy. When you break that routine, your brain scrambles. If someone tells me, "I just don't feel right," the first thing I tell them to do is get back on their routine. Your atomic habit should be the foundation on which you build this routine and the rest of your habits.

Before you try to overhaul your entire life, pick one atomic habit and stick with it. It should be something that starts your day off on a positive note, gets you in the right mindset, and contributes to your overall health and wellness. Chances are you already have something you're doing every morning. If so, grab onto that and make it a no-excuses habit.

If you don't have anything in mind, here are a few examples:

- Make a healthy breakfast—This is my personal atomic habit. I don't just pour milk over some cereal; I go all out. I fry russet potatoes and onions in olive oil, I cook sausage, make eggs, and make avocado toast, and eat it mindfully with a glass of grapefruit juice. I start my day with a solid plate of nutrition, and the half an hour it takes to cook, eat, and clean up all helps me set an intention for my day.
- Work out—A lot of my friends use workouts as their atomic habit. They wake up and hit the gym every single morning. A morning workout wakes you up, releases endorphins, and starts your day off productively. If you're already working out in the morning, it would be easy to make this your atomic habit.
- Meditate—We're going to talk (a lot) more about meditation in a few pages, but meditation is the definition of setting your mindset for the day. If this is your atomic habit, you can clear your mental plate and set an intention first thing in the morning.
- Get organized—The whirlwind of your day can leave you unorganized. If you wake up and just take 20 minutes to make your bed, tidy up your apartment, write a to-do list, and plan out your day, you're setting yourself up for massive success.

If atomic habits are new to you, I challenge you to just sit with that habit for a month or so. Don't try to go any farther, just promise yourself to do your atomic habit on good days, bad days, and everywhere in between.

One at a Time

When you've established an atomic habit, you can start to build off of that atomic habit. Solid habits repeated over years and years can become so engrained into your brain that they aren't even alpha-level brain activity anymore; they can sink down into theta activity. You wake up and can't help but perform them. When you have a positive habit that is *that* deep, the only limit to what else you can stack on top of it is how many hours you have in a day. When you stack a bunch of habits over your atomic habit, all of a sudden that neuroplastic pathway becomes an unstoppable neuroplastic super-highway.

I started with breakfast, but now my morning routine looks more like this:

- 7 a.m. -Wake up and shower.
- 7:15 - Get Dressed.
- 7:20 - Feed my cats.
- 7:21 - Make Breakfast.
- 7:45 - Clean my apartment.

- 8:05 - Meditate.
- 8:15 - Drink a coffee and write for an hour.
- 9:15 - Start work.

But these things don't happen overnight. You need to build your daily habits one at a time. Do not try to create a multitude of good habits all at once. Starting a good habit and breaking a bad habit both use up your reserves of beta-brain willpower. If you try to start five new habits all at once, your beta brain will only be able to give 20% of its power to each of them, and your current pathways will hijack those efforts and continue running old programs.

Instead, start with one habit and stick with it until you're satisfied it's on autopilot. If you're substituting a bad habit, depending on how deeply ingrained the bad habit was, it might take three weeks or it might take three months. Only you know when the process is complete. Eventually, when you notice yourself running your new, good habit on autopilot, you're ready to stack a new one on top of it.

Use Triggers and Rewards

In *The Power of Habit,* author Charles Duhigg discusses the use of triggers and rewards to substitute a habit. If you lay Duhigg's framework over the brainwave framework, you'll see that a trigger sets off your anticipation mechanism, which starts a process that leads to a reward. Repeated action of that circuit creates a habit as the initial beta-wave activity gets reduced to alpha-wave activity as your brain makes it all more efficient.

Duhigg's substitution mechanism lies in using the same trigger and the same reward (if possible) but substituting the process in between for a better habit. Triggers are incredibly useful for me. I try to use triggers that link to my senses to initiate habit loops.

One of these triggers for me is ambient lighting. I have a light in my office that has an adjustable light temperature setting. Early in the morning, the light temperature is much brighter and closer to daylight. Through repetition since birth, my brain has learned "white light = wake up time," and this light in my office only reinforces that. Later in the day, I change the light tone to an amber hue, which signals that I'm approaching bedtime. I make sure my computer has similar settings; from 7 a.m. to 7 p.m., my screens are blue light dominant, and from 7 p.m. to 7 a.m., they're amber dominant.

I also use my sense of smell as a trigger, because the sense of smell is closely linked with emotion and memory. If you've ever walked into Bath and Body Works and grabbed a candle, then immediately thought, "Wow, this one reminds me of a summer picnic with my mother when I was 10," this is why.

I might get a bad rap for this, but if you've made it this far, I'm going to confess something to you … I am an avid user of essential oils for this reason. I have different essential oils that I diffuse in my apartment depending on what part of my day I'm in, all to act as just one more trigger for my habits. In the morning, I diffuse a blend that contains peppermint to stimulate brain activity, and in the evening, I diffuse a blend that contains lavender to ease my brain into lower brainwave states toward sleep. Honestly, I have no clue whether peppermint or lavender have any causal effect compared to any other scent. I'm not claiming they do (although I can't imagine falling asleep to peppermint).

What I do know though is that when I sit down to write after my morning list of habits, I'm sitting in the same brightly lit area, the room is the same temperature, and I smell peppermint. I've set up at least three triggers to stimulate a habit process in my brain, and combined with all of my habits, I have no trouble writing a few thousand words every morning.

Once you make it all the way through the process, if you really want to solidify your habit, reward yourself for performance. Sometimes the performance of a habit itself results in a reward; for me, the act of eating breakfast itself is inherently rewarding (see our conversation about food above). If you enjoy your habits and you have them stacked in a logical order, moving on to the next habit in a stack can be a reward in itself. This is why some people call them waterfall habits; they start a chain reaction.

If the performance of your habit is not inherently rewarding, most people find checklists to give them a nice spike of dopamine. There's just something about checking off a box that you performed a task that acts as a reward, especially once you've built some momentum. Just don't fall into the trap of forcing yourself to perform every habit every day for the sake of those check boxes; if you end up here, your check box habit itself becomes a bad habit.

One Final Word

Don't become a habit addict. It is okay, even encouraged, to not perform your entire habit stack on certain days, especially if more pressing matters call your attention. Perform your atomic habit and move on; don't get addicted to the high of checking off boxes.

I used to think it was absolutely crucial to hit my entire habit stack every single day, or otherwise I was going to start a downward spiral. But then a friend pointed out to me that I was trying to implement all of these habits to ease stress, but I was causing myself more stress than I was easing by trying to nail every habit every day.

He was totally right. I was trying so hard to nail down all of these habits, that I was using a bunch of beta-brain power in doing so, which completely defeated the purpose of creating habits in the first place.

Don't make your good habits a bad habit.

MEDITATION IS A REAL THING

Whether you're substituting new habits into existing pathways or creating new habits from scratch, you'll probably hit a point where it all feels like a bit much. It's hard to get all of those systems on autopilot or even to recognize when they're on autopilot compared to when you're expending beta-brain energy to finish them off. How do you know what brain state you're in at any given moment? If you're in the wrong one, how do you change it?

The key to recognizing what brain-state you're currently in, and to controlling your movement between them, is having a solid meditation practice. There are certain cues that alert you to your current brain state, and meditation is all about learning to recognize them.

You might have tried meditation before and gotten frustrated. "I just get so bored … what's the point of sitting here and doing nothing?" I get that, but at the same time, I would tell you to learn to accept your boredom through meditation. But yes, I know it's frustrating because you don't see immediate results. You sit down, "meditate," and you just feel nothing.

That isn't how meditation works. To build the right pathway within the right brain state, your brain needs to be exercised repeatedly, just like your muscles do. Results are not instantaneous no matter how much we want them to be. If you want to build a muscle, you don't see results after one workout. You see results over time. You go to the gym every day for two months, and then when you look back at a picture of what you looked like, you think, "Woah, I look different."

Meditation has the same effect. You won't feel the immediate benefits, but you'll reap the rewards with a regular practice. Meditation is the action of slowly, day by day, learning to recognize your current mental state and widening and strengthening your conscious control within that state.

The best way to start the foundations of a meditation practice is to follow trained experts. None of us really know how to meditate starting out, and there are hundreds of fantastic meditation courses out there that will guide you through a meditation practice. But there is one I recommend, because it comes paired with a state-of-the-art piece of technology: the Muse Headband.

Muse is a consumer model EEG device that is capable of reading the electrical signals produced by your brainwaves and sending the results to your phone. Muse also comes with a meditation app that converts those signals into audio feedback, which trains you to recognize your alpha state through repeated meditations.

If your brain is in an active beta state or higher, you'll hear thunderstorms. While meditating, the Muse app directs you to focus on your breath. As your brain approaches a state of calm, the audio feedback starts getting quieter, and then if you manage to achieve a state of extended alpha brainwaves, you hear birds chirping, rewarding you for doing the right thing.

Sound familiar? Cue (start meditating) process (focus on breath) reward (bird chirping). You're actively training your puppy. The headband conditions you to know what brain state you're in and learn to recognize it.

This audio-neuro feedback, combined with the hundreds of meditation programs available through the app, will help you fast track your learning.

What happens when you meditate

In the meantime, if you want to try a meditation on your own, it's incredibly simple. All you have to do to get started is set aside 10 to 15 minutes, find a comfortable position, and bring your attention to your breath. For ten minutes, focus on the sensation of breathing wherever it is the most prominent to you. It could be your nostrils, stomach, chest, wherever you feel the sensation of the breath.

Whenever you find your mind wandering, make a mental note. You don't need to linger on it, and do not punish yourself for your wandering thoughts. Just think to yourself "oh, interesting, I got distracted again," and return to your breath. Curiosity about what distracts you from your focus helps you identify what pulls you away.

If you've never meditated before, I encourage you to take ten minutes now and complete your first meditation before reading on. If you're an avid meditator, think back to your first meditation.

How was it? Were you able to focus on your breath for the entire time? In … out … in … out … for ten minutes? I highly doubt it, unless you are some type of zen master. More than likely, your mind wandered. Hopefully you noticed, and it probably went something like this:

What was that noise? I bet it was the neighbor's dog … that dog is always making noise. Oh, interesting. I'm distracted. Back to my breath.

Why does my back hurt? I didn't even notice that. What muscle is that? Why can't I sit in this position for ten minutes without my back hurting? Distracted. God dammit. Wait, don't punish yourself. Interesting. Back to my breath.

Counting breaths. One … two … three … is it possible to get distracted from my breath by counting my breath? I wonder how long I'll go this time … Distracted. Time to start over at one.

Distractions can be anywhere. Maybe it's a pain in your body, maybe it's a noise, or more often, it's internal. Whatever distractions pop up during your ten-minute meditation session are those same distractions your internal puppy is always dragging you toward, and you are actively training your mental puppy not to chase them.

Habit substitution can only go so far; your puppy will continue to drag you off track and toward something else. Maybe there's an email that's making you anxious, or maybe a problem in your life that needs solved. Whatever it is, your brain is frequently distracted from whatever it is you're supposed to be focusing on.

But hopefully, you recognized that you were distracted for a second and made a conscious effort to return your focus to your breath. This action of recognizing the distraction, over and over again, is what strengthens your brain. You're building that neuroplastic pathway in your brain that says, "Hey, it's okay to be distracted, but maybe let's return to what the conscious brain wants to focus on." You're training your puppy to sit and stay.

TRANSFERRING YOUR MENTAL STRENGTH

Having strength in this area of your brain can be transferred to literally any other thing you could possibly wish to pursue. The idea that your conscious brain is as focused as possible on the task you want to be focused on, that you aren't distracted, and that you are fully present is what's known as mindfulness. Mindfulness can be practiced always, and it's all about being in the present. You're not distracted by the past, or the future, but are centered on what is happening **right now**.

The power of mindfulness is immense. Before I stumbled upon the practice, I never realized how little control I had over the thoughts in my head. But at this point, I've been meditating and attempting to institute mindfulness practices in my life for roughly one year, and my productivity, focus, and overall life contentment increased. I also noticed that when I let myself slip—when I feel back into my mindless habits, stopped meditating as much, and generally lived my life without focus, I was irritable and pursued unhealthy habits.

The best thing about a mindfulness practice is that once you've established the base of your practice, you can practice mindfulness anywhere and everywhere.

You can practice mindfulness in the gym. Pre-mindfulness, you might try to finish your set and scroll through your phone until the next one. 10 reps, Facebook, repeat. With mindfulness, you can attempt to be fully present with your body and limit distractions. "Is this the correct form? Am I cheating in any way when lifting this weight? Am I using a muscle that I'm not supposed to be using? What does that feel like? Is this weight too much? Too little?" Thirty seconds of breath control between reps. Repeat.

Or when you're doing yoga, you can focus on your breath and get two benefits for the price of one: you can do a full body stretch and tension release while building your mindfulness practice. Fully focusing on the sensation of a muscle stretching while practicing deep breathing has the same effect as focusing on your breath.

However you choose to do it, whenever you're going through a stack of habits, you can choose to make it a mindful activity. I applaud you if your atomic habit is making breakfast, but if the entire half an hour you're anxiously awaiting work emails, you're still in the beta-brain state. If you've successfully programmed a habit loop, but your brain is constantly distracted by what's coming next, you're only halfway there. Instead, allow your brain's autopilot to take control, and let your beta brain watch your alpha brain work with curiosity and interest.

"Look at that golden retriever go. He's being so good. I don't even have to tell him what to do."

Mindfulness in the alpha state is important, and being able to control your mind and your own thoughts has a powerful effect over every other thing you will do in your life. I've found that in attempting to achieve my goals, I am my own worst enemy. My tendency to get distracted, focus on something else, and never reach my full potential is what holds me back. Mindfulness is a tactic that helps me reach that goal, no matter what my goal is.

The goal isn't really to reach this state of pure unadulterated focus for the rest of your life. You'd be kind of weird if you did. The goal is to simply reach a point where you're capable of switching it on and off, like a tool you have at your disposal. It is okay to be distracted, and you have to accept that. Because if you can't accept your failures, you won't make progress.

To wrap up this section, here's what we've learned.

- Repeating the same action causes a habit, and you can substitute out good habits for your bad ones.
- Anything you do every day can be put on autopilot to reduce the amount of decisions you're forced to make in a day.

- A consistent meditation practice strengthens your neuroplastic pathways, makes room for more habits, and trains your inner puppy to be quiet while your habits are at work.

Now you're ready to move on to beta-level activity.

THE BETA BRAIN

You probably have a project you're working on that requires a ton of brainpower. I have no data to back this, but I feel pretty confident saying that people who read self-development books have passion projects, and they want to get them done.

Anyway, getting this passion project done is all about exerting your beta-brain willpower toward that goal. Good news, if you've established a meditation practice, you've already done the hard part.

In a past life, I used to be a painter, and as a painter, the hard work was in the preparation. If I wanted a paint job to last, I had to clean the surface, make sure there were no underlying problems, and apply some primer before I started painting. But even before that, I had to communicate with the customer and my crew, pick up the right color paint, make sure everyone had supplies, and check the weather to make sure it wasn't going to rain. Slapping a coat of paint on the house was the easy part, but the actions I took before any paint went on the house were 90% of the journey.

The same principal applies here—90% of the work required to go into a deep state of concentration is in the preparation. If you've done all of the preparation in the previous chapters, if you've reduced the amount of brain power you exert on a daily basis by turning your every-day decisions into habits, and, if through the power of meditation, you've strengthened your ability to focus on one thing, you're ready to do some work.

What Is the Beta State

The best description of the beta-brain state comes from the book *Deep Work* by Cal Newport. In short, deep work is the ability to focus without distraction on a cognitively demanding task. And Newport agrees with how to get there:

> The key to developing a deep work habit is to move beyond good intentions and add routines and rituals to your working life designed to minimize the amount of your limited willpower necessary to transition into and maintain a state of unbroken concentration.

In his book, Newport argues that a fulfilling life is a deep life, and a deep life is one where we have room in our day to concentrate thoroughly on our passions without distraction. In a world full of constant notifications, we're trained to be distracted as our default state. But true fulfillment and meaning, he argues, are found when you throw all of your unadulterated energy into your passion, free of distraction. Newport calls this "going deep."

Deep work happens in the beta-brain state. Specifically, it happens in the mid to high beta bands, where your dominant brainwaves oscillate between 15 and 38 hertz. It's when your brain is so consciously enthralled with creating something or solving a unique problem that there are no other distractions. Not your email, not your phone, not your cat or your wandering thoughts.

I won't repeat Newport's work here—understanding the true value of deep work should come from the source itself, and I highly recommend that you read his book. But for now, just trust me that those who make deep work a habit often more than double their output. The year Cal Newport made deep work a habit, he published eight academic papers, more than double his previous output. The year I made deep work a habit, I got a 4.0 in law school and business school simultaneously, across 10 different graduate courses. (This was not the norm for me.)

True impact comes from making deep work a habit. You already know how to create a habit ... so all I really need to do is give you a few beta-brain specific tips.

Getting into the Beta State

Whether you know it or not, you already have a solid routine to get into the beta state. The process of waking up in the morning is just a process of moving through the brain states. While you're still asleep, your brain moves from its lowest frequency of activity, the delta state, up to theta brain state—from deep sleep to dream sleep.

Then the first thirty minutes after you wake up, your brain is in a very unique alpha state that's still clinging to unconsciousness. In low-alpha, you're a walking zombie, and your brain isn't ready to make decisions yet. Don't do anything important during this time, just accept what is and begin the process of waking up. I use this time to take a shower, get dressed, and start making breakfast. After eating breakfast and drinking a cup of coffee, I have the fuel I need to use a lot of brain power, and my morning dose of caffeine is another boost toward that beta state.

Even before I consciously realized what I was doing, my morning routine was designed to push me up toward the beta-brain state from sleep. I slowly but surely go from movement, to thought, to fuel, to energy, all the while moving up in brain waves. You probably do too.

If you want to make going deep a little easier, I recommend the following tricks:

1. *Go Deep First Thing in the Morning* - Our brains and bodies work in accordance with our natural circadian rhythm. That little pattern I mentioned above isn't just a coincidence; every human is like that. From about 30 minutes after you wake up to two hours after that, your brain is in peak beta-state. It makes sense that if you have a big decision to make that requires a lot of brain power, you should make that decision before you expend too much of that brain power. If you wait until 4 p.m. to try to solve your day's biggest problem, you've already expended most of your beta-brain energy for the day and have reached decision fatigue. It just isn't going to work. So, if you have a project that requires a deep level of concentration, be it writing, problem solving, or something where you should not be disturbed, do it first thing in the morning. If you can't, studies have shown that an extended break containing a meal have lowered decision fatigue in the afternoons. Eat a snack.

2. *Stack Deep Work on Top of Your Atomic Habit* - When I say do it first thing in the morning, I mean do it right after your atomic habit. One of the biggest problems people have when it comes to deep work is that they only work when they're motivated to. But motivation strikes at random times, and it never stays. Motivation is what causes you to have started twenty projects yet finished none of them. Discipline,

on the other hand, finishes projects, and discipline is built through repeated action. I found the discipline to finish this book by stacking the deep work of writing right after my morning habit stack. My habit stack was designed to help optimize my brain power during peak beta-brain time, and like every other repeated action, the more often I sat down to write the easier it got. Now it's just second nature. If you add deep work into your morning habit stack, your daily habits will become the trigger you need to start this work, and over time, you'll be a disciplined deep-work aficionado.

3. *Meditate and Breathe* - It's inevitable that when going through your morning habit stack, your mind will wander. Early in the morning, your brain *wants* to concentrate on something, and sometimes your mind will wander to the point where it starts to beta-level concentrate on the wrong thing before you sit down to work. I'll be cooking breakfast and listening to a podcast on NPR when suddenly, "*Hmm ... man, if Congress would just ...*" and my beta-brain is off to the races, deep in thought on the *wrong* topic. If I didn't let go of that thought, on top of all my other distractions, my brain's attention would be divided amongst my goal, my plan for congress, what my cat is doing, and the need to return that amazon package sitting on my desk before 30 days is up.

But to prevent this, I'll do a breath meditation.

Pro-tip: I highly recommend that if you're going to drink coffee in the morning, you do your meditation *first*. I find that caffeine speeds up my beta state, but it also makes my brain latch on to whatever I happen to be thinking about at the moment, and it's almost impossible to stop. If I'm thinking about work emails in the morning and I drink a coffee, I will end up addressing work emails.

But by focusing on my breath for 10 minutes, I use a little bit of that brain power, but it allows my brain to just clear out my short-term memory to the point where I can choose what to focus on. At the end of ten minutes when the meditation bell goes off, your mind should (in theory) be fairly blank. Make sure the first thing that pops into your head is that passion project and get to work.

Side Tip: If you want to take it one step further, you can incorporate some special breath work into your meditation. Did you know that at any given time, about 90% of the air you breathe goes in and out of only one of your nostrils? Your nostrils switch off every few hours, but at any given time, one side of your brain is getting more oxygen than the other. If you force yourself to breathe through both nostrils for a few minutes, it will help to fully oxygenate your brain. I prefer to use a certain school of *pranayama* breathing, where you breathe in one nostril, out the other, reverse and repeat for three to five minutes. This helps clear out your nasal passages, oxygenate your brain, and, if you're fully focused on the breathing, gets you into a good alpha brain state, just before jumping up to beta.

4. *Limit Distractions, Repeat.*

    Once you get into a state of deep work, the key then is to just stay in it. If you're new to deep work, it's really difficult to work on a project for two hours straight with zero distractions. You'll feel a natural urge to get up, check your phone, get a snack, or browse the internet. Even if you don't feel that urge, you might just stare at your computer (or other problem) not knowing where to start.

    But like every other habit, exercise builds strength. If this is your first time and you manage 20 minutes of deep work, I would call that a success. You'll only build this habit if you set yourself up for success. Just like building your atomic habit, making deep work a habit is another thing where you can train your brain into sitting still. For me, this meant placing my cell phone in another room and disconnecting from the Wi-Fi. Otherwise my little puppy would run toward distraction.

    Give yourself some time. Rome wasn't built in a day.

THE NEGATIVE EFFECTS OF BETA STATE

Ok, if I master these habits and deep work, I'll just be able to spend more and more time in a beta-brain state and create a cycle of constant productivity, sleep, repeat.

At first it seems like the answer is yes. Gaining control of your consciousness isn't something that happens in a day. Depending on where you started, it can take years of effort to get all of your habits in alignment and to get to a state where you are capable of two straight hours of deep work. For those years, you'll be stacking more and more brain power.

But eventually, you will hit a point where, no matter who you are, any additional beta-brain activity is harmful to you. I am not a psychologist. That being said, I am going to briefly touch on the topic of anxiety here, but if you think you have an anxiety disorder, I suggest you talk to a licensed therapist.

Let's revisit the topic of decision fatigue. When you're in a high-beta brain state, you're constantly making decisions. During writing, I find myself in a high-beta state (my Muse headband is full of thunderstorms). This makes sense, because essentially, I'm in a state of constant decision making, because there is no pattern my brain can automate to write a book like this. I am constantly making decisions about what comes next, what I think the reader will find interesting, and whether it all makes sense. Every sentence is a new decision.

Every day that I sit down to write, I find that I can only write for about an hour before I am just mentally exhausted and need to take a break. The constant decisions wear my brain out.

Even someone who's practiced deep work for a long time only has two solid hours of deep work in them at any given time before they need to take a long break. I'm not talking five minutes, I'm talking a break long enough for you to relax, eat some food, and allow your brain to get down into the alpha-brain state.

But there are a lot of information workers out there, myself included, who have to do a lot of mentally taxing work a day more than just two hours. Some people might drink an additional coffee and try to push themselves to make more and more decisions. Others stack endless deadlines in front of them so that they are motivated by the fear of missing the deadline. Either way, you're training your brain to constantly be in beta state, and this is actually really bad for you.

Have you ever had one of those days where you have no choice but to work for 10 to 12 hours straight? You're pushed up against a deadline, and you just have to constantly expend that beta-brain power, no exceptions? Try to recall what happens after you've completed your task.

For me, I find it almost impossible to calm down. I get stuck in this ineffective, disorderly beta state where my thoughts are running a mile a minute with no logical pattern. Often times, I'll develop a headache, and I'll have trouble falling asleep. And when I do finally fall asleep, my sleep quality is low. It's like my brain is STILL running around in that jumbled mess, and I'll wake up multiple times during the night, often from a dream about whatever I was working on.

Now imagine having to work 10 to 12 hours a day in the beta-brain state, every single day, constantly making decisions. Decision fatigue is still present, but eventually, like everything else, your brain will even automate making decisions. (Remember the inmates seeking parole who were less likely to be granted parole at the end of the day?)

Constant beta-state activity is the definition of burnout. You make decisions until you just can't anymore, and then you're done.

Researchers have found in multiple studies that those diagnosed with anxiety disorder, especially those experiencing symptoms of an anxiety attack, show high levels of beta-brain activity, and there is significant evidence for the fact that prolonged periods of beta-brain activity can lead to declining mental health outcomes.

There are a lot of other factors that put pressure on knowledge workers. There is external stress and deadlines, and there is often an incredibly competitive environment. But my hypothesis is that the imposition of prolonged states of beta-brain activity on workers such as lawyers, doctors, accountants, and graduate students is a significant factor in what leads to lower mental health outcomes.

What I'm trying to say is this—you only have so much decision-making power in you. If you force yourself to stay in the beta state for too long, you will likely start to experience anxiety and decreased effectiveness. And if you're already experiencing anxiety and decreased effectiveness, you should meditate and find your way to an alpha-brain state and allow your brain to rest.

In the end, finding balance will work out in your favor. Thomas J. Stanley, author of *The Millionaire Mind*, surveyed 1,300 millionaires and found an interesting fact: those individuals at the very top of the class were less likely to be millionaires, and those that fell in between the top 10% and 20% of the class were the most likely to end up millionaires.

You probably knew some of these people at the top of the class, and for me I always wanted to be like them. Constantly studying, constantly disciplined. But really, they were forcing their brains into a constant beta state, and they did not have balance in their lives. Constant beta-brain activity is NOT the answer. There is more to a successful life than work.

The goal is not to spend all day in a state of deep work. The goal is to make the most out of your two hours of deep work, and structure your day in a balanced manner between all of the brain states. You could try to go all out for a few months and expend endless brainpower, crash, and burn out. Or you could stack small wins for two hours a day over the years. Finding balance between all of your passions will lead you to a fulfilling life.

STRUCTURE YOUR DAY AROUND YOUR BRAINPOWER

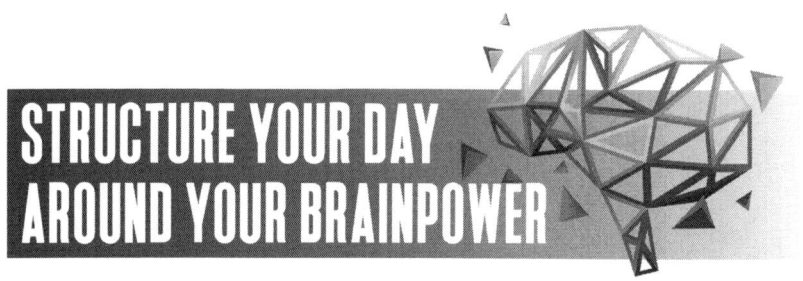

If you want to be the most efficient, from the time you wake up to the time you go to sleep, you should structure your day around where your brain naturally falls at certain times. If you have the luxury of controlling your schedule, you can perfectly structure your day around your brainpower. If you don't, hope is not lost; simply do your best with what you have.

As always, you will never stick to a perfect schedule. But progress is better than perfection—just do your best. My idea of a perfect day, structured around my brain power, looks like this:

1. Wake-up Routine—Start with your morning routine, and go through your habit stack, whatever you chose that to be. Never sacrifice your atomic habit, but make sure your morning habit stack doesn't last longer than an hour before you get into deep work.

2. Deep Work—Do your deepest work first thing in the morning, right after your habit stack. About an hour after waking up, your brain is sufficiently aroused, but you have not yet expended a bunch of decision-making power. You are ready to make the difficult decisions. If you're a knowledge worker, this is when I suggest your hardest, most focused work, such as document drafting, writing, or difficult research—any of those projects where you know you just need a good two hours to get them out of the way. After about two hours, when you reach that point of mental exhaustion, take a 15- to 30-minute break.

3. Mid-Beta Work—Remember how beta waves are divided into three bands? You should start your day in the highest beta state, where you need to make the most decisions. But that doesn't mean the rest of your day is useless. You have plenty of other work to do that doesn't require as many decisions on your part, and that work happens in lower beta bands. This could be research, where you have come up with a work product where you already know the answer and you just need to confirm it. Or it could also include responding to emails, reading, or essentially any work that doesn't require a massive amount of decision-making power on your part.

4. Long Break—After you've finished a mid-beta task, your brain needs a break. At this point in your day,

you've probably been working for three to four hours, and your brain needs an hour off. In the study on decision fatigue involving judges, the judges were found to have an uptick in decision making after taking a break to eat food. So, take a break, eat your lunch, and if you have the luxury, take a 30-minute nap. After you've returned, you can continue doing mid-beta work.

5. Low-Beta Work—At some point between 2 to 4 p.m., you'll hit a point where you've expended a majority of the brain power you have at your disposal, and you just can't bring yourself to do any more brain-expending work. This is the best time to schedule your low-beta work, such as meetings, conference calls, or that work that just doesn't take much energy. For me, significant portions of my job involve copying information from hundreds of documents into spreadsheets. This is perfect low-beta work, because all I have to do is look for the piece of information, think "Yep, it's there," and hit copy-paste. No brainpower required; I just follow the rules that are already set.

If you've gotten here, your *work* is done for the day, but your brain isn't. Your day isn't over, and it's time to transition into a different brain-state.

YOU NEED TO CALM DOWN

To make the most out of your beta-brained productivity, you need to find balance in your life between each of the brain states. If you attempt to spend all of your time in the beta state, you will become less and less effective until eventually you can't bring yourself to do anything. You need to come down out of that mentally taxing brain state and recharge.

Most people have a wind-up routine, but you also really need a wind-down routine.

By this point, I hope you trust that your brain can only do so much in a day, and balance is the key to a healthy brain. But your brain won't just turn off automatically. If there is no break in between your decision-making work and bed, your brain will just keep running the same loops over and over again in an exhausting cycle.

You need to do something to get your brain back down into an alpha-brain state. So, you already have a wind-up routine to get into beta state, why not have a wind-down routine to get out of it? Just like every other habit you have, your brain will start to carve a pattern, and you will wind down automatically if you use the same trigger for your "I'm done here in beta state, time to wind down" routine.

I highly suggest the trigger for your wind down routine be some form of physical activity or working out.

"Absolutely not, I go to the gym first thing in the morning every day."

Alright, I get it, but just hear me out. Have you ever thought about why you go to the gym first thing in the morning? It's probably because when you first got into a work-out routine, you had to go in the morning or else you wouldn't go at all, and you just never changed that habit.

For those who've never had a workout routine, it takes a lot of brainpower to get yourself to go to the gym and perform unpleasant physical exertion. For those people that have not made physical fitness a habit, going in the morning is a good suggestion because that's when you have the brain power at your disposal to head to the gym. You need to use that brain power just to finish the workout. So, if you don't already have a gym routine and are trying to start one, then you have an excuse. I'll let you go to the gym in the morning.

But you people who are gym-junkies, who've been going for years, you have no excuse. Those morning hours are prime beta-brain productivity hours and lifting weights doesn't require a bunch of difficult decisions. It's an alpha-brain activity. You've gotten to the point where exercise is one of the best parts of your day, and you know you're not going to miss your workout. If you're at this point, making the decision to go to the gym isn't hard for you, and I suggest you go in the afternoon as part of your wind down routine, to get a solid chunk of alpha brain activity in right after a long work day.

And here's the cherry on the cake—your body would rather work out in the afternoon as well. Just like your circadian rhythm works so that your decision-making power is greatest in the morning, your *body* is strongest in the afternoon. Assuming you wake up around 7 to 8 in the morning, your body is the most coordinated around 2:30 p.m., your reaction time is best around 3:30, and your muscle strength and cardiovascular efficiency is best right around 5 p.m.. Don't believe me? Look it up—most Olympic records were set in the afternoon. So, if not for the brain power, move your work-out routine to the afternoon just for the gains.

Having a solid wind-down routine is one of the most important things you can do, and exercise is one of those things where you can "get in the zone," AKA the alpha-brain state. In addition, exercise releases a lot of positive brain chemicals, and has been shown time and time again to reduce depression. A lot of people wind-down with a glass of wine… but I suggest substituting that with a healthier habit with positive side effects. Throwing weights around and jamming to some music is the perfect transition from hard work into your evening relaxation.

After your workout, the more you can let your brain relax in the evening the better. You don't have to do anything specific, just something that isn't mentally taxing. At the same time, I also suggest something you can get absorbed in, like a really good TV show or a book.

There's something to be said for getting lost in someone else's story. You can use your beta brain to create, but when your beta brain needs a break, you can slow down and take time not to create, but to consume something that someone else has created.

If you really think about it in depth, you would never be able to create anything without consuming the work created by others before you.

What I'm trying to say is this: just stop working. Don't feel guilty for it. You don't need to be productive every single moment of every single day. I used to feel guilty watching TV or reading nonfiction books. I want to make a huge impact on the world, so I need to constantly be working at making that impact, right?

Wrong. What the world really needs is balance. And when you look within yourself, you will find that you will make the biggest impact on the world when you yourself have found balance.

TRANSITIONING INTO UNCONSCIOUSNESS— THE THETA STATE

Have you ever heard that the goal of meditation is for your mind to go completely blank? I always thought this was kind of a load of bullshit. My mind is NEVER blank. I am constantly thinking about something.

But as we've seen, even our own thoughts can distract us from our passions. And in meditation, we learn to slow the onslaught of those thoughts. Slowing those thoughts has its own benefits, such as gaining the ability to focus on one thing for an extended period of time.

But if you get good enough at slowing down the thoughts, it's possible that there's a point where there are actually no thoughts in your consciousness. So eventually, I discovered that "going blank" wasn't complete and total bullshit.

On a Tuesday afternoon after I had finished my work, I decided to do a body-scan meditation. If you've never done a body-scan meditation, I highly recommend it—the goal is to relax every muscle in your body, which in turn relaxes your mind.

If you have a lot of stress, or work out often, or both, your body will start to hold a lot of tension. Your shoulders will creep up, your back muscles will constantly tense, and a lot of people even find that they're constantly holding in the need to use the restroom. All of this tension builds within your body to the point where if your brain isn't the distraction, the aches and pain in your body will be. If you ignore these signs long enough, you'll end up getting sick. Your body will just shut down.

The purpose of a body-scan meditation is to direct your attention to each muscle in your body, one at a time, and consider whether that muscle is holding any tension. You start at your feet and work your way up your body over half an hour, releasing each muscle until your body is completely relaxed.

After you've done this quite a few times, you'll learn to start releasing muscles you didn't even know you had control over in your body. This might sound incredibly weird, but I swear to god I've gained the ability to release the pressure in my sinuses on command after a body scan.

Once you've released all of your body tension though, you're ready to get into a fantastic meditative state.

That afternoon, I was wearing my Muse headband, and I was in the middle of a guided body scan meditation. When you do these extended meditation practices, often your guide will give you 5 to 10 minutes of silence within that meditation. And at the end of the body scan …

My mind just went completely blank.

It was such a bizarre experience for me that I find it difficult to describe. I was focusing on my breath, and I had absolutely zero distractions. But it wasn't like I was controlling my breath either, I felt like I was watching it from a distance.

And for about five minutes, I was hovering in a state that was perfectly balanced between sleep and wakefulness. And at the end, when the meditation guide came back, I snapped out of it and thought, "Wow, what was that?"

I checked my Muse app and it registered almost no brain activity.

If you've conquered alpha-state meditations, and you've limited every distraction both internally and externally, you can sink down into the theta-brain state.

Why am I telling you this?

Honestly, I don't know that there are a ton of benefits to being in a conscious theta-brain state. In the theta-brain state, you achieve stronger benefits of alpha-state meditations, such as relaxation, and give your beta brain a break and time to recharge. Going completely blank and just dumping all of your worldly thoughts is just refreshing.

But the reason I'm telling you this is that the little spot, right between alpha state and theta state, if you can train yourself to enter that spot on demand, then you can guide yourself to sleep.

The transition from alpha to theta is the gateway to sleep.

SUCCESS HAPPENS OVERNIGHT——THE DELTA STATE

kind of mean that in the literal sense, in the fact that sleep is absolutely crucial to your own success.

Are you one of these people?

I only sleep four hours every night and I m perfectly fine.

Research shows that only about 1 in 8,000 people can sleep less than eight hours a night without any negative effects, and it's because those people have a very specific genetic mutation.

A lot more than one in 8,000 people are claiming to be "fine" on less than eight hours of sleep a night. And while those people might claim to be fine, they're only fine because their mental capacity and their daily output of productivity is not decreasing from the point it's at now.

But it's not improving.

If you want to learn the true impact of a good night's sleep, I highly recommend the book *Why We Sleep*, by Mathew

Walker, a leading neuroscientist and sleep researcher. In his research, Walker has found evidence linking sleep deprivation to cancer, diabetes, Alzheimer's disease, obesity, and a whole host of mental health problems. In addition to that, a lack of sleep negatively affects the process by which your brain converts short-term memories to long-term memories.

In short, your body and your brain use sleep to repair themselves (and in the case of the brain, to improve itself), and when you deprive yourself of that, you're depriving yourself of that opportunity to improve.

You won't be surprised to learn that this process is linked to your brainwaves, specifically the theta- and delta-brainwave states.

But before you drift off to sleep, the process of falling asleep starts with alpha waves. In countless hours of sleep studies, sleep scientists have found that the brain state preceding sleep is consistent alpha rhythms, and this makes sense, because alpha rhythms are the brain's natural state of relaxation. If you've ever laid awake in bed at night, thinking about work, or that embarrassing statement you made in eighth grade, your brain is still producing beta waves and is still too active and awake to drift off to sleep.

But as you get more and more relaxed, your brain will transition down from the alpha-brain state to the theta-brain state. Unless you're actively meditating, somewhere in this transition between alpha and theta is the point where your conscious brain lost control of your mind, and you "fell asleep."

When you hit this point, your eyeballs will start to slowly roll around in your eye sockets (called "slow rolling eye movements"). Slow rolling eye movements are an external marker that show that your brain is predominantly in the theta state.

After about 20 minutes in the theta state, your brain will fall down into the delta state, and then forty to sixty minutes later, you will come back up into the theta state.

So why am I telling you all of this?

While each state has a host of functions, theta state works more predominantly on your brain, and delta state simply shuts your brain down to give your body an opportunity for repair. But the theta state is crucial to mental improvement: it has been shown to host the process by which short-term memory is transferred to long-term memory.

In his research, Mathew Walker conducted a study on college students that drank alcohol before bed. Alcohol is a known inhibitor of the theta-state process of memory transfer.

Walker had the students learn a set of information, with the expectation that those students would be tested on that information after they slept. As expected, the students who did not drink alcohol tested better than the students who did drink alcohol.

But the surprising thing that we see in Walker's study is that the brain codes short-term memories into long-term memories over a span of seven days, not just the same day.

Walker ran a series of tests where students learned the information on Monday, with a test on Friday. One set of students did not drink alcohol during the week, and another set of students drank a large amount of alcohol on Wednesday night.

Despite having two full nights of sleep on Monday and Tuesday without alcohol, and again on Thursday night, the students who drank alcohol on Wednesday scored *40% lower* on the Friday test. What this shows is that the process of converting the new material that you've learned during the week can be inhibited by a reduction in theta-state REM sleep at any point during the week, not just the day you learned it.

You need to get good sleep every night, not just certain nights.

So why do I need to sleep for eight hours during the night

During the night, your brain goes through four to five sleep cycles. During your first sleep cycle, your brain spends most of its time in the delta-brain state. Our brains have no conscious control over the delta state (which is kind of the whole point of the delta state to begin with). In delta, your brain's control over the body is completely and totally shut off, and it gives your body time to repair the muscles and tissues that were damaged during the day. This makes sense, because evolutionarily, it is more important to repair the body than it is to convert memories, so body repair should be the priority.

Our ancestors would rather run from predators than solve calculus problems.

But as we go through sleep cycles, the ratio of theta to delta sleep changes, and we get more theta sleep in the later sleep cycles. Theta state sleep, or REM sleep, is the state in which you experience dreams. Have you ever noticed that you tend to wake up in the morning from a dream? That's not necessarily because you just *forgot* about all of the dreams you had earlier in the night, it's because most of your dreams occur after already getting a good night's sleep. From about sixth hour of sleep to the eighth hour of sleep, your brain is predominantly in the theta state, where you experience dreams and convert short-term memory into long-term memory. You experience dreams right before waking up because your brain has finally finished repairing your body and can start work on your mind.

If you're only sleeping for six hours a night, you're missing that last crucial sleep cycle in which your brain spends most of its time in the theta state. You're missing that round of sleep where your brain converts your short-term memories into long-term memories. You might wake up with your body being refreshed, and that's because delta state did its job. But theta state never got its moment.

So, if you spent hours and hours the day before learning new information, you're wasting your time if you aren't getting eight hours of sleep, because a little less than half of the information you learned won't be encoded into long term memory.

That conversion to long-term memory is what makes this entire process a system. It's where the habits are made. It's where your mental highways are built. It's what makes your brain more efficient and puts systems on autopilot.

That's why you need to get eight hours of sleep.

So, if you're one of those people that thinks, "Man, if I only sleep four hours a night, I'll have an extra four hours to improve myself," know that getting that extra four hours of sleep is really what cements your daily improvements into your long-term memory.

The entire point of this chapter is this: nothing else I've covered in this book means anything if you're not getting enough sleep. Sleep is nature's medicine. If you're looking for some miracle cure, look no further than your own bed.

Use the Tools You Have to Fall Asleep

If you've implemented the practices in this book up to this point, you already possess all of the tools you need. They key to falling asleep is being able to shift out of the beta-brain state and into lower and lower frequencies of the alpha-brain state, until eventually you hit theta state and fall asleep. (And if you're an experienced meditator, conscious meditation down into the theta state is the key to lucid dreaming, but that's not what this book is about).

Sleep is absolutely crucial to every other part of your well-being. The work you accomplish in the beta state, your ability to build systems and habits, and your ability to improve will be diminished if you aren't getting enough sleep.

So, to round out your day, I suggest that you do everything you learned in the first chapter of this book to make sleep a habit. Put your sleep habits on autopilot. Use the color of the lights in your bedroom and an essential oil as a trigger for your mental processes that it's time to go asleep.

And like everything else, practice it over and over again until it's on autopilot. Every night when you go to bed, do another alpha meditation. If you have a Muse S Headband, it even contains a program for sleep meditations to guide you off to sleep.

Eventually, even the process of falling asleep will become more of a system, reinforcing the system that is your entire day.

PUTTING IT ALL TOGETHER

Now it's on you. You have most of the tools you require in your life to pursue balance, and if you take nothing else away from this book, I hope you've taken away the fact that balance is exactly what your brain needs to be the most productive.

You might beat yourself up for what you perceive to be laziness. Whether that's taking a break, watching TV, or getting a full night's sleep, we want to constantly be productive, and to me, that used to mean that I constantly needed to be in a beta-brain state.

But after years of trying to maximize my productivity by just pushing through it all, I've learned that constant presence in the beta state is exhausting, even sickening. Your life instead should become a pursuit of balance.

Your morning routine will ground you for the day; it creates a sense of normalcy and checks off the items that are required to bring you health.

The time you spend in the beta state gives you purpose. You will do your absolute best to channel your beta state productivity toward things that you believe are going to change the world for the better. When you accomplish these items, it gives you a sense of fulfillment.

But every day, you will hit a point where you're just out of energy, and you have to learn to accept that. Your workout routine can transition you from the beta state back down into the alpha state to clear your mind.

And the relaxation afterward, that's the time you can spend for yourself, just enjoying the fact that you're alive.

And eventually, you drift off to sleep, where your body repairs itself from the tasks of the day, and your brain takes all of the new information you've learned and encodes it in an efficient manner, making it ready for recall.

You can repeat this system for the rest of your life and be completely and entirely fulfilled.

But there is one last piece of this—the one that I really call a superpower—that I want to share with you.

THE EUREKA STATE

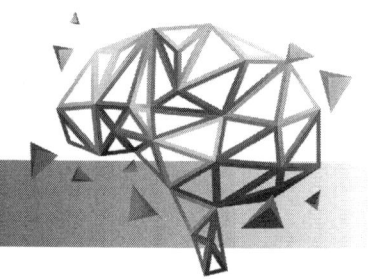

The ability to just google things on command with the supercomputer in our pockets has really ruined the eureka state.

Have you ever tried to remember someone's name …

"It's on the tip of my tongue, don't tell me … don't tell me … SCOTT MEYERS. THAT'S WHO IT WAS, SCOTT MEYERS."

This is the eureka state in action. The eureka state is actually the gamma-brain state, and it's the brain state we know the least about. Gamma brainwaves are associated with moments of sudden insight, where an answer just comes to you out of nowhere.

I'll be honest with you here, when you're wearing an EEG device, the electrical signals that an EEG picks up from your brain could definitely stand to be more accurate. It takes two to three seconds of consistent signals for an EEG to pick it up, because the electricity needs to be detected through layers of skin, your skull, and amid all sorts of other interference. This is really hard to do.

We know so little about gamma waves because they're the highest frequency brainwaves (over 50 Hz), and they come and go in an instant. The sheer moment of recognition is all that it takes for you to experience a gamma wave. And because of that, only the best medical grade EEG devices will pick them up.

Although the science is relatively new, we've figured out that what happens when gamma waves are present is that many different pieces of your brain experience a strong electrical signal, almost like a shock. It's like your ENTIRE brain is working together to give you the answer to the question you seek.

But gamma waves rarely appear out of nowhere; there's a secret to making them appear.

In his book *The Eureka Factor,* John Kounios expertly explained the science of insight, slightly before we really knew how gamma waves even worked. Most humans understand the concept of a eureka moment, and his explanation was based off the stories of those experts who had reported eureka moments before massive revelations. Every eureka moment had a pattern to it, and it went something like this:

(1) Work really hard on something, to where you're holding all of the pieces of the puzzle in your mind;
(2) Take a break, and it will come to you in a moment of insight.

Sound familiar?

Achieving a eureka moment is simply a matter of doing a lot of deep work in the beta state, holding all of the pieces of the problem you're trying to solve in your head, and then backing down into the alpha state.

Our brains are wired for it, and once you back down into the alpha state, your subconscious will solve the problem and deliver it to your conscious brain in the gamma state. Our brains are always trying to make things more efficient by aligning the knowledge we learn with the knowledge we already know, and weeding out conflicts.

When you hold all of the pieces of the puzzle in your mind, if you tell your beta brain to be quiet for just a second the subconscious will work its magic and start stacking that knowledge into your memory bank. After a moment of relaxation, it will resolve the conflict between the pieces of information in your brain and deliver it to you on a silver platter.

Time for a confession:

I live for eureka moments. Sudden realization and insight is like a high to me, and the entire reason I started working on this book in the first place was to figure out how to get more of it.

Of course, I came to realize that the key was finding balance between all of my brain states, and here we are.

But there is one interesting thing I discovered along the way ... which is what I like to call the Eureka Vacation.

No matter what you do, as time goes on you will find yourself beginning to hold large amounts of tension.

Whether you're a consistent meditator, or you do a lot of yoga, or whatever it is, eventually the responsibility and stress of life will start to build.

It starts with tension in your brain. You can do your best to prolong the mental fatigue using the methods in this book, but eventually you'll start hitting a point where you're just tired. No matter how well you execute on your to-do list, it seems never-ending.

Then eventually, the tension will start to manifest in your body.

From working out, or sitting at your desk, or general stress, you'll find that your muscles will constantly be holding tension. What I mean by this is that certain muscles (many times specifically the shoulders, neck, upper back, and various leg muscles) are constantly active and never actually hit a state of relaxation.

Imagine your muscles have electricity going through them. The most intense workout of your life is a state of 100% electricity in your muscles, and a state of complete and total muscle relaxation is 0%. When tension builds, your muscles hit a point where they operate at a constant of 20%, even when you're sleeping.

The state of constantly holding tension will compound to cause further issues. You won't get a good night's sleep because you'll wake constantly throughout the night to reposition yourself due to cramps, which inevitably leads to decreased sleep quality, which leads to lack of focus.

The mental and physical tension will start to build to cause other forms of tension. It will seep into your life in other ways—mental irritability, lack of focus, anxiety about work, and lack of organization. Maybe your apartment starts getting dirty and disorganized, and you start getting snippy with your spouse.

If you're getting dangerously close to not hitting your waterfall habit every day (or if you've missed it), you need a break. You need to decompress.

I've only found one solution to this, and it has an almost ritualistic form. You need a eureka vacation.

The eureka vacation can't happen at just any time; it needs to be planned. You can take just a weekend for your eureka vacation, or just a day or two off work, or maybe you take a week-long vacation. But whatever you choose, you need to follow a process.

When I say a eureka vacation needs to be planned, I mean you need to plan it around completing your beta-brain deadlines and knocking all of your nagging items off of your to-do list.

Plan your eureka vacation for a time when you know you're going to complete a big project. Maybe you've finished a months-long task at work, or you just finished a semester of school.

Whatever it is, your eureka vacation should mark a transition from one period in the pursuit of your passions to the next period. A time to drop everything.

When you've found a good finishing point for your major projects, the second part is that you need to make people aware that you're taking some time off (even if it's just a weekend). The last thing you need is to finish one big project and then jump right into the next one without a break. Remember: Your brain needs balance.

Before you start your eureka vacation, though, you need to do what's arguably the most painful part—swallow your frogs.

A good friend of mine came up with this analogy—swallowing frogs—for tasks that you just do not want to get done. Frogs usually aren't related to your main pursuits, but they're those nagging, low priority items, that when left unfinished, can become a thorn in your side. Things like filing your taxes, renewing your license plate registration, or completing a task you said you'd do months ago that's been on your back burner.

A good indicator that a task is a "frog" is if you think about it and can say, "I've been meaning to get to that … but I keep putting it off."

The day after you finish your big passion project, use your prime beta-brain power of the next morning to knock out all of the frogs on your list.

Bam. Now you're ready for the next state. At this point, there should be nothing else nagging at you mentally that you need to get done. Your big project is done, your frogs have been swallowed, and you can release the tension in your brain.

The next thing I advise you to do is release the tension in your environment. For me, as the tension builds over the months, evidence manifests in my apartment.

After I've knocked out my frogs, I'll clean the entire house, top to bottom. Laundry, dishes, countertops, floors. I'll make it spotless. It's just one more thing that your brain can stop focusing on as a "thing I need to do."

At this point, ask yourself. Is there something else in your brain on your to-do list? Is your brain saying, "You can't take a break before you get this done"?

If so, you won't get to your eureka vacation. Finish it and come back.

The goal of a Eureka vacation is to relax in a guilt free manner. If you can look around and say "man, I've been meaning to do that," or "yeah, this needs done," you're not ready.

When all of your outer tensions are absolved and your to-do list is empty, it's time to look inward.

When your house is sparkling clean and you've taken a shower and changed into the most comfortable clothes you own, you should already be feeling more peaceful. There is nothing around you that "needs done."

Now, I'm going to suggest you deviate from your normal routine. Chances are, you've spent a majority of your day swallowing frogs, tying up loose ends, and cleaning your apartment (or traveling, if you're taking a destination eureka vacation).

I want you to stay up past your bedtime to enter the eureka state. I find that if I start the last part of this little ritual past my normal bedtime, my brain is already slightly off its routine. It's relaxed, but at the same time it's not following a pattern. It's thinking, "Hmm … this is different, what's going on here?"

At this point, all of your external tension should have been resolved, but your body is still holding that 20% internal muscle tension. It's time to relax that.

Start with just breathing.

In. Out. In. Out. Nothing more.

When you're holding tension in your body, generally something starts to hurt after those three to five minutes. Try to focus on the breath. Eventually, if you're sitting completely still, you will hit a point where the pain is too intense. Start by completely stretching that muscle.

For example, the last time I did this, my most painful muscle was my upper trap, the one right in between my neck and my shoulder. So, I stretched that first. I would roll my head ALL the way around, complete 360, full range of motion. What I noticed is that as I stretched one muscle, another muscle would call my attention. Then I'd stretch that one, and the next one, and the next one, and eventually I would identify a type of muscle system …

If you're holding tension in one part of your body, it will spread to your entire body. The upper neck muscles are supported by the traps, which are supported by the delts and the lats. If the upper neck is tense, the traps compensate to hold your head up, and then the lats compensate to hold up your traps. Eventually this will cause problems in your lower back, and your glutes and hamstrings will compensate in those areas … and suddenly your whole body is tense. If you're holding tension, every part of your body is working too hard to try to help another part of the body. You need to reset.

So, for at least an hour, I advise you to focus on completely, totally relaxing each and every muscle in your body where you can feel tension. While you're releasing muscle tension, focus on your breath, and find the added benefit of sinking down into the alpha-brain state.

Do this for your entire body, then sit still and repeat. If after five minutes you feel pain again, continue to stretch. Repeat the cycle until you no longer feel any pain.

Eventually, you find the root of your physical tension. If you keep chasing the muscle pain through your body, eventually you'll feel a muscle that has been holding tension for **months** finally release. It's unlike any feeling you've ever felt before. Your brain is already in the alpha state, but when you release your last piece of body tension, your brain goes completely silent, registering the lowest brain state on a Muse headband.

When you identify the root muscle that causes the tension, the body system is complete.

When you hit this point, you reach a point of complete, utter mental clarity. For me, I am instantly full of energy, and my brain immediately identifies the path forward.

If you've gone through the entire ritual, think about what you just did: You just spent months working toward a passion project that you completed, and then a final day or two holding all of the pieces of a giant project in your mind in the beta state.

But then you checked off every item on your to-do list. You released all of your mental tension, you released the tension in your environment, and then you released the tension in your body.

You just went through the entire ritual to hit the gamma state.

When I finally reach this point of clarity, I can see with ease the things that are causing me the most pain and contributing the most to my tension, and I come up with a plan to prevent those items at the start of my next big project. When I hit this point of clarity, I am 100% confident, without a shadow of a doubt, that the plan I have concocted is the best way for me to move forward.

WHERE TO GO FROM HERE

No matter what your goals are (whether you want to become an all-star business person, or a politician, or if you want to lose weight or get in shape, or make better connections with your friends), you'll always be better at your goal if you're in tune with who you are as a person—if you're in tune with your brain.

Of course, other pieces and parts of your life are absolutely crucial to your wellbeing, but by definition, you can't function without your brain. Without your own psychology—without whatever it is that goes on in your conscious that makes you, well, you.

But it's not *just* your brain. If you died, we couldn't just put your brain in a jar and be like, "Voila, this is Thomas" (or whatever your name is).

No, what we *are* is much deeper than that. What are we? Why should we even care what we are?

Knowing who you are, at a deep, neurological level—knowing the definition of the word "I" is incredibly important to finding and defining the purpose of your life and making an impact on others.

What am I? What is the "self?"

A lot of people think "the self" is whatever you want it to be. That's kind of an inspiring thought, right? "I am whatever I choose to be." And to an extent, it's true. You can choose to define what you are, but there are limits. We live in a world where there are constraints.

While you can choose what you want to be, you, as a human cannot choose to become something that, by the laws of physics, it is impossible to become. You cannot just one day decide to be a tiger. It just doesn't work that way.

You can choose to be what you want to be within the constraint of being a human being. But as we've seen, even our brain has its own internal constraints.

Within all of these constraints, how do you choose what you *want* to be? If you were born in a room devoid of sensation, no light, no sound, no smell or touch or temperature to sense, what would you want? How does your brain even develop the thoughts that lead you to think, "I am whatever I choose to be"?

Your brain has to learn what things are before it can learn that it wants them. If you were born and lived in a vacuum, void of light or any sensory input, your brain would never know what it even means to want. Your brain has to have a foundation to build upon before it can recognize the fact that it is more than just a brain; it is a conscious thing, with goals and wants.

What you want to be is influenced by the sensory inputs experienced by your brain.

All of these sensory inputs have occurred from the moment your consciousness came into being until now. Everything you've ever experienced, including reading this very sentence, has the opportunity to form your consciousness and influence what it means to "want" something.

This process starts chemically, but as you have seen in this book, we can learn to control it.

When you ask, "What am I?" When you define the self—when you "choose" who you want to be—you are choosing to take a particular action within the context of all of the actions the brain has taken so far, and within the chemical processes that the brain uses to process those actions. You can make the choice, but only within these limits.

Most philosophers who've really done a deep dive into this question agree, with minor differences, that the definition of "self" is the combined result of what you do.

You are the sum of your actions.

The actions you have taken in your life so far create your own conscious definition of what you are. And based on that definition, you can make a conscious decision to control your future actions toward a purpose of your choosing.

Your "self" up to this point is concrete. You can't change it. But from this point to the end of your life, you have the ability to change and control what the "self" becomes, because you can choose to take actions that shape your mental experiences in the way you want them to be shaped. So, the question then, is:

What do I want to become?

If you're not completely clear yet on what your purpose is, that's totally okay. You shouldn't really expect yourself to be able to completely identify your life's purpose, because as you learn and grow, you will prune and shape that purpose.

We tend to discuss the goal of humans as striving for happiness. In general, life is suffering, and we attempt to take action to ease that suffering, in the opposite direction, toward happiness. Even today, as I write this book at my desk with multiple computer monitors, in my climate-controlled house, iced coffee in hand, I can **still** say that my goal in life is to ease suffering toward states of higher and higher levels of happiness.

But how will you personally do that? What is your purpose?

Do you know the answer to this question? If you're like me when an ethics professor first asked me this question, then you probably haven't even thought about it, let alone come up with an answer. But I want you to think about this for just a few minutes. What is your ultimate purpose? Why are you on this planet? Why were you born?

That may be getting a little too philosophical, so let's back up. Why did you pick up this book? Why read a book that professes to give you the tools you need to use your brain in a more efficient manner if you don't know why you want to do so in the first place? What are you working toward? Where are you trying to go? What are you trying to do?

Once you define your purpose, making progress can be boiled down into a semi-simple formula. Once you have a purpose, you can then create a goal toward your purpose. "*I am here, and I want to be there.*" The goal is nothing but a metric by which you can measure progress toward your ultimate purpose, and the way you are heading between points A and B is your "direction." Finally, once you have goals set in the direction of your purpose, you can break those goals down into smaller actions. *If I repeat this single task on a consistent basis, I will reach this goal.*

Throughout the journey that is your life, your purpose may change, and that's okay. At some point, you may learn that your "purpose" was actually just a goal and that you were subconsciously following your purpose in pursuit of that goal. But what I want you to see is this: that if you lack direction toward a purpose, you will have no idea what goals to set. If you have no idea what goals to set, you have no idea what actions to take, and if you can't take any actions, then you're stuck.

You might be thinking at this moment, "My purpose is to be good at my job," whatever that job may be. Some people would refer to this as a calling, such as "my purpose is to pursue my calling as a doctor." But a *calling* doesn't answer every single question. A calling is a powerful thing; it is the best means by which you can pursue your purpose.

That's exactly what I thought it meant to have a purpose when an ethics professor first asked me the question. I remember sitting in his ethics class, 95% of the way finished with a law degree and an MBA simultaneously, cocky and smug, thinking to myself that my purpose was to be the best lawyer in the world.

But then we did a quick, simple exercise in his class, which really helped me discover what my true purpose was.

The exercise consists of two parts:

(1) Write your own eulogy.
(2) Consider what you will regret when you die.

If you've never completed this exercise, it's really mind blowing. Take the place of one of your closest friends or relatives, maybe your spouse, your child, your parent, or your best friend, and write down what you think that person would say about you if you died today. Take five to ten minutes to write down one-page worth of material.

Make the experience as realistic as possible. Close your eyes and imagine a room full of your closest friends and family. Once you've set the scene within your brain, take out the eulogy you've written and read it out loud. Knowing your friends and family, what would they be thinking during the reading of your eulogy?

Then do the hardest part. Circle everything that *isn't* true. Think about what you've written—is it true? Did you write a eulogy that really embodies who you are, as a person? That includes all of your faults? Or did you write a eulogy that is just a little *too* perfect? Would one of your closest friends be sitting in the audience and think, "No, that's a lie"?

The purpose of this exercise is to show you how you want to be viewed by others when it really matters. When it's all said and done, how do the people who care about you the most look at you as a person?

Next, take a few moments to ponder your internal thoughts at your death. Imagine yourself in a comfortable place. Maybe in your bed, or on the couch at home, covered in a blanket. Or maybe you're sitting in front of a fire, or you're sitting on the beach, watching the waves roll in, watching the sunset. You watch the sun start to dip below the horizon. And you realize that the sun in its current state represents your life right now. It's not over, but it's nearing completion.

Imagine the best parts of your life. From growing up, to becoming a young adult, through finding a life partner, or many friends to share your life with. And imagine what you've accomplished in life. Take 30 seconds to reminisce on the absolute best moments of your life.

You feel the warm rays of sun on your face. You can hear the waves lapping at the shore. You are completely, and totally, relaxed. Your best memories are starting to fade away, as you begin to focus on the sound of the waves.

If you had to change one thing about your life, what would it have been?

These two exercises are extremely powerful. It's not often in the hustle of everyday life that we, as seemingly far from death as we are, ponder what we will love and regret about our lives in the end and how those who care about us will view us the day we die.

Draw your own conclusions as to what it all means. How can you apply how others felt about you on your dying day to your actions today? How can you take a step today to create a "best moment" that you will look back on in the sunset of your life? What can you do now to prevent that final regret?

From experience in doing this exercise, and from experience in reading the best moments and regrets of those approaching the end of their lives, they tend to fall into two categories.

The first category is "I wish I would have spent more time with those I love," or in the positive, "My best moments were those I spent with the people I love." This idea can be heard countless times throughout our society, for example, *"you'll never regret the day you didn't spend in the office."*

The second category is "I wish I would've made the impact on the world that I knew I was capable of making," or in the positive, "My best moment is when I accomplished _____," and these accomplishments usually have a large, meaningful impact.

So, what do we get out of all of this?

For me personally, what I got from this knowledge and doing this exercise was that the most fulfilling thing you can pursue in your life is balance. If your best moments are those you spent with family, you may regret that you didn't have a bigger impact on the world. If your best moment is a huge accomplishment you achieved at work, you may regret the time you didn't spend with family.

I view balance between two extremes as the best path. Science tells us that happiness is a balance between caring for yourself and caring for others; and that makes complete and total sense.

After all of this, my purpose is advancing humanity by helping others, in a way that helps myself.

And I encourage you to use your brain to its fullest potential to achieve that purpose.

ADDITIONAL READING

Knowledge is not invented, it's discovered. It has always existed, someone just had to figure it out and share it with everyone else. This process of discovery is only possible by learning the knowledge that has come before us.

This book would not have been possible without the knowledge I got from the following books and programs. I highly recommend that you read these works, as I consider these authors the masters and myself the student. This book would not have been possible without them.

- *Incognito* and *The Brain* - David Eagleman
- *Hacking the American Mind* - Robert Lustig
- *The Power of Habit* - Charles Duhigg
- *Atomic Habits* - James Clear
- *Grit* - Angela Duckworth
- *The Inner Game of Tennis* - Timothy Gallwey
- *Irresistible* - Adam Alter
- *How Emotions Are Made* - Lisa Feldman Barrett
- *Deep Work* - Cal Newport
- *Why We Sleep* - Matthew Walker

- *The Eureka Factor* - John Kounios
- *The Four Tendencies, Outer Order Inner Calm,* and *The Happiness Project* - Gretchen Rubin
- *The Three-Day Effect* - Florence Williams

ACKNOWLEDGMENTS

A lot of people went into making this book happen so I would like to thank:

1. My wife Tory for supporting me on the days I want to be a writer, the days I want to be a lawyer, and the days I don't want to be anything.
2. Jantzen Mace, for the never-ending conversations that end with the words "you should write a book about that."
3. Gary Williams, for helping me turn a cosmic cloud of ideas into a somewhat cohesive solar system.
4. The Incubator Team, for getting me through the book manuscript.
5. The Frog Squad, for actually getting me through the book manuscript.
6. Aaron Griffin and Andy Nardone, for always picking up the phone and listening to my rants.

7. The Fall Execution Team, for pushing me to just publish this thing already.
8. Mom and Dad, for pushing me to always be one step above where I was yesterday.
9. Riley Suter, for being a great editor.

ABOUT THE AUTHOR

Logan Bryant is an attorney in Cleveland, Ohio and author of *Master your Mind: How to Control Your Mental State Instead of Your Mental State Controlling You.* Logan is a self-professed self-development junkie, having read over 300 books prior to writing one, all with the goal of drawing on the power of the world's expertise to solve problems. When not working or writing, Logan spends time with his wife, Tory, and his two cats, Splat and Moscato.

Can I Help You?

After finishing this book, I don't really know what I want to do next. I want to expand on this idea, but have no clue where it's going to take me. Did reading this book spark an idea in your brain? Something that you would like to talk about? Something I can help you with?

Call me. I'm serious. 330-635-8322. Let's talk about it.

Can You Help Me?

Thank You for Reading My Book!

I really appreciate all of your feedback, and
I love hearing what you have to say.

I need your input to make the next version of
this book and my future books better.

Please leave me an honest review on Amazon letting
me know what you thought of the book.

Thanks so much!
Logan

Made in the USA
Middletown, DE
11 July 2021